The Lichtenberg Figures

The Lichtenberg Figures

BEN LERNER

COPPER CANYON PRESS

Cover photo by Bert Hickman, Stoneridge Engineering

Copper Canyon Press is in residence at Fort Worden State Park in Port Townsend, Washington under the auspices of Centrum Foundation. Centrum is a gathering place for artists and creative thinkers from around the world, students of all ages and backgrounds, and audiences seeking extraordinary cultural enrichment.

LIBRARY OF CONGRESS CATALOGING-IN-PUBLICATION DATA

Lerner, Ben, 1979–
  The Lichtenberg figures / Ben Lerner.
     p. cm.
  "2003 Hayden Carruth Award."
  ISBN 1-55659-211-6 (pbk. : alk. paper)
  1. Sonnets, American. I. Title.
  PS3612.E68L53 2004
  811´.6—dc22

                              2004006038

COPPER CANYON PRESS
Post Office Box 271
Port Townsend, Washington 98368
www.coppercanyonpress.org

ACKNOWLEDGMENTS

Grateful acknowledgment is made to *Aufgabe, The Beloit Poetry Journal, CROWD, Denver Quarterly, The Paris Review, Ploughshares, Post Road, Slope, 26, Verse,* and *Web Conjunctions,* where some of these poems first appeared.

Thanks to Ariana, C.D., Keith, Brady, Jon, Forrest, Max, Rishi, Rosmarie, and my family for their many forms of support.

for Eric, Ed, Stephen, and Cy

§

The dark collects our empties, empties our ashtrays.
Did you mean "this could go on forever" in a good way?
Up in the fragrant rafters, moths seek out a finer dust.
Please feel free to cue or cut

the lights. Along the order of magnitudes, a glyph,
portable, narrow — Damn. I've lost it. But its shadow. Cast
in the long run. As the dark touches us up.
Earlier you asked if I would enter the data like a room, well,

either the sun has begun to burn
its manuscripts or I'm an idiot, an idiot
with my eleven semiprecious rings. Real snow
on the stage. Fake blood on the snow. Could this go

on forever in a good way? A brain left lace from age or lightning.
The chicken is a little dry and/or you've ruined my life.

§

I had meant to apologize in advance.
I had meant to jettison all dogmatism in theory and all sclerosis in organization.
I had meant to place my hand in a position to receive the sun.
I imagined such a gesture would amount to batter, battery. A cookie

is not the only substance that receives the shape
of the instrument with which it's cut. The man-child tucks
a flare gun into his sweatpants and sets out
for a bench of great beauty and peacefulness.

Like the girl my neighbors sent to Catholic school, tonight
the moon lies down with any boy who talks of leaving town.
My cowardice may or may not have a concrete economic foundation.
I beat Orlando Duran with a ratchet till he bled from his eye.

I like it when you cut the crust off my sandwiches.
The name of our state flower changes as it dries.

§

In my day, we knew how to drown plausibly,
to renounce the body's seven claims to buoyancy. In my day,
our fragrances had agency, our exhausted clocks complained so beautifully
that cause began to shed its calories

like sparks. With great ostentation, I began to bald. With great ostentation,
I built a small door in my door for dogs. In my day,
we were reasonable men. Even you women and children
were reasonable men. And there was the promise of pleasure in every question
we postponed. Like a blouse, the most elegant crimes were left undone.

Now I am the only one who knows
the story of the baleful forms
our valences assumed in winter light. My people, are you not

horrified of how these verbs decline—
their great ostentation, their doors of different sizes?

§

What am I the antecedent of?
When I shave I feel like a Russian.
When I drink I'm the last Jew in Kansas.
I sit in my hammock and whittle my rebus.
I feel disease spread through me like a theory.
I take a sip from Death's black daiquiri.

Darling, my favorite natural abstraction is a tree
so every time you see one from the highway
remember the ablative case in which I keep
your tilde. (A scythe of moon divides
the cloud. The story regains its upward sweep.)
O slender spadix projecting from a narrow spathe,

you are thinner than spaghetti but not as thin as vermicelli.
You are the first and last indigenous Nintendo.

§

We must retract our offerings, burnt as they are.
We must recall our lines of verse like faulty tires.
We must flay the curatoriat, invest our sackcloth,

and enter the Academy single file.

Poetry has yet to emerge.
The image is no substitute. The image is an anecdote
in the mouth of a stillborn. And not reflection,
with its bad infinitude, nor religion, with its eighth of mushrooms,
can bring orgasm to orgasm like poetry. As a policy,

we are generally sorry. But sorry doesn't cut it.
We must ask you to remove your shoes, your lenses, your teeth.
We must ask you to sob openly.

If it is any consolation, we admire the early work of John Ashbery.
If it is any consolation, you won't feel a thing.

§

I attend a class for mouth-to-mouth, a class for hand-to-hand.
I can no longer distinguish between combat and resuscitation.
I could revive my victims. I could kill a man
with a maneuver designed to clear the throat of food. Tonight, the moon

sulks at apogee. A bitch complains to the polestar. An enemy
fills a Ping-Pong ball with Drano and drops it in the gas tank of my car.

Reader, may your death strictly adhere to recognized forms.
May someone place his lips on yours, shake you gently, call your name.
May someone interlace his fingers, lock his elbows, and compress your chest,
every two seconds, to the depth of one and one-half inches. In the dream,

I discover my body among the abandoned tracks of North Topeka.
Orlando Duran stands over me, bleeding from his eye. I can no longer distinguish

between verb moods that indicate confidence and those that express uncertainty.
An upward emergency calls away the sky.

§

Pleasure is a profoundly negative experience, my father
was fond of saying underwater. His body was carried out
like a wish. We paid our last respects
as rent. The mere possibility of apology allows me to express
my favorite wreck as a relation between stairs
and stars. I take that back. To sum up, up

beyond the lamp's sweep, where a drip installed by heat
still drips—some tender timbers. At thirteen, I had a series
of dreams I can't remember, although I'm sure
that they involved a rape. I'm brutal because I'm naked,
not because I'm named, a distinction
that the scientific and scholarly communities,
if not the wider public, should be expected to maintain.
No additional media available (but isn't it beautiful when a toddler manages to find and
    strike a match).

§

I invite you to think creatively about politics in the age of histamine.
I invite you to think creatively about politics

given men as they are: asthmatic, out of tune and time,
out of bounds and practice. I invite you to run your mouth, to run your hands
through my thin hair like a theme. I invite you to lean your head

against my better judgment. Once uncertainty
ran through these sketches like a Lab. Now, of my early work, a critic has said:

"It was open, so I let myself in." Ladies and gentlemen,

tonight's weather has been canceled. The Academy has condemned
the blue tit. The poor are stealing the saltlicks. Grenades luxuriate
in the garden of decommissioned adjectives. It is the Sabbath. I must invite you

to lay down your knowledge claims,
to lay them down slowly and with great sadness.

Given men as they are, women pack snow into jars for the summer ahead.
Given men as they are, the trees surrender.

§

I'm going to kill the president.
I promise. I surrender. I'm sorry.
I'm gay. I'm pregnant. I'm dying.
I'm not your father. You're fired.
Fire. I forgot your birthday.
You will have to lose the leg.
She was asking for it.
It ran right under the car.
It looked like a gun. It's contagious.
She's with God now.
Help me. I don't have a problem.
I've swallowed a bottle of aspirin.
I'm a doctor. I'm leaving you.
I love you. Fuck you. I'll change.

§

True, a great work takes up the question of its origins
and lets it drop. But this is no great work. This is a sketch
sold on the strength of its signature, a sketch
executed without a trial. Inappropriately formal,

this late work reflects an inability to swallow. Once
my name suggested female bathers
rendered in bright impasto.
Now it is dismissed as "unpronounceable."

Polemical, depressed, these contiguous black planes
were hung to disperse museum crowds. Alas,
a generation of pilgrim smokers
has arrived and set off the sprinklers.

True, abandoning the figure won't change the world.
But then again, neither will changing the world.

§

for Ronald Johnson

The sun spalls the sluiceway into shards.
The blind man finds an equivalent for adult films.
The rabbi downs a hin of wine and gives

it a rest. A votive candle is delicately set
into a small, decorative paper bag
weighted with sand and placed in a row
along the dock. The poet will never walk
again. Not even in poems.
Lightning bugs set down their loads.

Tonight the women have the feel of men
who've worked. For you I have retired a word.
It is the only word that never appeared in your books.
It was the only word you didn't know.
It begins with the letter *O.*

§

To forestall a suicide, I plant all manner
of night-blooming genera. I compose this preemptive elegy.
I describe the sky as "noctilucent." In this very elegy,
the sky is thus described.

To prevent slow singing, I rub the body down
with acacia. I pledge to hide
the man who struck the body. I threaten to use
the same rope or opiate but minutes after.

To keep the neighbors from delivering all manner
of sympathy casserole, I water the Scotch.
I hide the Drano. I no longer park
in the garage.

I discover the body prone, check its breathing.
Go back to sleep.

§

I confused her shadow for an accent.
I confused her body for a simplified prose version of *Paradise Lost*.
I confused her heritage for a false-bottom box.
I confused her weeping for express written consent. "Choked with leaves"

is the kind of thing a child would say in this rhomboid fun park and yet
you've been saying it under your breath, way under, ever since
the posse of stars rolled in. Obese with echo, Milton tips his brim.

Twenty-one years of destroying all evidence of use has produced extensive evidence of wear.
So I hike up my graphite trousers and set out
for an epicenter of great beauty and peacefulness. "A major event."
She called the publication of a portable version "a major event."
She called my adjusting the clasp "a major event."

She confused my powerful smell for a cry from the street.
She confused exhalation for better living through chemistry.

§

I must drive many miles to deliver this punch line.
I must drive many miles in the modern manner,

which is suicide, beneath this corrigendum of a sky. Tonight
Orlando Duran went crazy. He smeared every doorknob,
lock, and mirror in his apartment with spermicidal jelly.

To expel air from the lungs suddenly

is not to live beautifully in the modern manner. Rather
one must learn to drive, to drive
in the widest sense of the word, a sense that seats four
other senses comfortably. Tonight Orlando Duran

delivered himself in the modern manner,
delivered himself like a punch line. Is this what he meant by

"negative liberty,"
by "the sound of one hand clapping is a heartbeat"?

§

Possessing a weapon has made me bashful.

Tears appreciate in this economy of pleasure.

The ether of data engulfs the capitol.

Possessing a weapon has made me forgetful.

My oboe tars her cenotaph.

The surface is in process.

Coruscant skinks emerge in force.

The moon spits on a copse of spruce.

Plausible opposites stir in the brush.

Jupiter spins in its ruts.

The wind extends its every courtesy.

I have never been here.

Understand?

You have never seen me.

$

The sky is a big responsibility. And I am the lone intern. This explains
my drinking. This explains my luminous portage, my baboon heart
that breaks nightly like the news. Who

am I kidding? I am Diego Rodríguez Velázquez. I am a dry
and eviscerated analysis of the Russian Revolution.
I am line seven. And my memory, like a melon,
contains many dark seeds. Already, this poem has achieved

the status of lore amongst you little people of New England. Nevertheless,
I, Dr. Samuel Johnson, experience moments of such profound alienation
that I have surrendered my pistols to the care of my sister, Elisabeth Förster-Nietzsche.

Forgive me. For I have taken things too far. And now your carpet is ruined.
Forgive me. For I am not who you think I am. I am Charlie Chaplin

playing a waiter embarrassed by his occupation. And when the rich woman I love
enters this bistro, I must pretend that I'm only pretending to play a waiter for her amusement.

§

The abolition of perspective is an innovation in perspective.
Found matter invades the middle distance.
Yet long after perspective has rigidified
perspective is propped up and televised. As if the painter
were an epiphenomenon of gesture. For many years,

we lacked an adequate theory of decline
and affected spiritual gloom
with a turbulent cross-layering of brushwork.
Then, with the invention of the camera, we began to cry.

Here a woman emerges from the surface plane, invites our gaze,
and disappears. Here a woman succumbs
to her own frenetic coloration. The pictorial attack

on closed systems is a closed system.
Found matter invades the middle distance.

§

When a longing exceeds its object, a suburb is founded.
Goatsuckers spar in the linden. The redskins are hunted.
When the hunt exceeds its object, the past achieves
pubescence. History pauses
for emphasis. After these poems are published,

money will be no object.
Money will be a gray bird known for mocking other birds.
The stars will be adjusted for inflation
so that the dead can continue living
in the manner to which they've grown accustomed.

When a dream of convenience begins to dream itself,
the neighborhood's last bamboos reel in their roots.
The children make love "execution style,"
then hold each other like moments of silence.

§

Your child lacks a credible god-term, a jargon of ultimacy.
He fails to distinguish between illusion (*Schein*) and beautiful illusion (*schöner Schein*).
He is inept and unattractive.
Today I asked your child to depress

the right pedal, to stop the action of the dampers
so that the strings could vibrate freely. In response he struck me
in the stomach with a pipe.

Your child is a bereavement arbitrarily prescribed,
a hyperkinetic disorder expressed in chromatic variations.
By the age of twenty-three, your child will be bald
and dead. He's a bright boy and eager to learn. But bourgeois spectator forms

have supplanted the music of the salon,
inciting a sheer vertical sonority
that has dispatched the theme to keys beyond his reach.

§

Resembling a mobile but having no mobile parts,
my instrument for measuring potential differences (in volts)
is like a songbird in a Persian poem. I have absolutely no

idea what I'm saying. I know only
that I have a certain sympathy
for the rhetoric of risk and mystery. Think of my body

as a local institution. Think of my body
as a monocoque. Think of my body
as the ponderous surgeons of Wichita

ready their nibs. When the first starlings began to cough up blood,
the night applied its cataplasm. The moon issued its scrip
to the Austrian dead. An expert described your son

as incapable of some really important shit.
Your son described his name in the air with a spliff.

§

They can take your life, but not your life signs, my father
was fond of saying after apnea. But that was before articles
shifted during flight, before our graphs
grew indistinguishable from our appetites. In fine,
that was the greatest period of American prosperity

since my depression. Father's left hand was an extension
of liberal thinking. It could strike a man without assuming
a position on the good. His left hand was a complete
and austere institution. In fine, it could move through

my body's DMZs without detection. But that was before
articles copped pleas and feels from objects, objects
rendered fulgent by our theories, back before my mood

swung slowly open
to let this ether enter like a view.

§

The poetic establishment has co-opted contradiction.
And the poetic establishment has not co-opted contradiction.
Are these poems just cumbersome
or are these poems a critique of cumbersomeness?

The sky stops painting and turns to criticism.
We envy the sky its contradictions. We envy the sky
its exposed patches of unprimed canvas
and their implicit critique of painterly finish.

It is raining for emphasis. Or it is raining emphases
on a public ill-prepared for the cubist accomplishment.
Perhaps what remains of innovation
is a conservatism at peace with contradiction,

as the sky transgresses its frame
but obeys the museum.

§

"Gather your marginals, Mr. Specific. The end
is nigh. Your vanguard of vanishing points has vanished
in the critical night. We have encountered a theory
of plumage with plumage. We have decentered our ties. You must quit
these Spenglerian Suites, this roomy room, this gloomy Why.
Never again will your elephants shit in the embassy.
Never again will you cruise through Topeka in your sporty two-door coffin.
In memoriam, we will leave the laws you've broken broken."

On vision and modernity in the twentieth century, my mother wrote
"Help me." On the history of structuralism my father wrote
"Settle down." On the American Midwest from 1979 to the present, I wrote
"Gather your marginals, Mr. Specific. The end is nigh."

I wish all difficult poems were profound.
Honk if you wish all difficult poems were profound.

§

for Benjamin

Sensation dissolves into sense through this idle discussion,
into a sense that sees itself and is afraid. Still, we must finish our coffee
and partition epiphany
into its formative mistakes. Reclining on my detention-camp pallet,

I dream in Hebrew of a cigarette
that restores immediacy to the theoretical domain.
Or, if that strikes you as immodest, I purchase a portable classic
and interpret it loosely
until the infinite takes place. Recent criticism understates

the importance of our coffee,
how it removes transcendence from beneath our pillows
and leaves us a pointless enigma or silver dollar in its stead.

The stars are a mnemonic without object.
Let the forgetting begin.

§

for Benjamin

The forgetting begins.
Infinitives are hewn from events.
The letters of your name fall asleep at their posts.
The dead vote in new members. Police declaw your books.

A suspicious white powder is mailed to the past,
forcing its closure. In order to avoid exposure,
I use the present tense. Sense grows sentimental
at the prospect of deferral. The stars dehisce.

By "stars" I mean, of course, *tradition,*
and by "tradition" I mean nothing at all.
A pronoun disembowels his antecedent.
Stop me if you've heard this one before.

Your body is broken by exegesis.
The thinkable goes sobbing door-to-door.

§

for Benjamin

The thinkable goes sobbing door-to-door
in search of predicates accessible by foot.
But sense is much shorter in person
and retreats from chamber to antechamber to text.

How then to structure a premise like a promise?

The heroic negativity of pleasure
is that it makes my body painfully apparent,
a body that weighs six hundred pounds on Jupiter
and next to nothing here in Europe.

How then to justify our margins?

Some cultures use quotation marks for warmth.
In ours they've withered without falling off.
The trees apologize each autumn,
but nature can never be sorry enough.

§

What, if not the derivative, will keep us warm? The tragic interchangeability of nouns?
The breastbone? Two vanguards sharing a bathroom?

When I first found the subjunctive, she was broke and butt-naked.
Now she wants half. She wants her own set of keys
and bullets designed to expand on impact.

A pamphlet of sparks? The National Book Award?

Meaning is a child of my third marriage. A marriage of convenience.
A wartime marriage. We had plastic champagne flutes and no champagne.
A staple instead of a ring. A dialectician in place of a priest.

A butter substitute? Rogaine for women?

Consider the rain my resignation. I regret having founded Cubism.
I regret the lines I broke by the eye
and the lines I broke by the breath.

The hair around the vulva? Proust in translation? September 11th?

§

Announcing a late style as distinctive as the late style of Matisse,
my grandfather no longer speaks.
The figure in my grandfather's memory has disappeared completely.
It has been replaced with a kind of allover abstraction
made up of broad and colorful strokes. Critics agree

that my grandfather's exaggerated midsection and useless legs
constitute a critique of consumer society,
that his body's adoption of chance procedures
signals a rejection of his former realist sympathies.

"The progressive surrender of the resistance of the medium
and the exclusion of all techniques extraneous to the medium"
is one way to conceive of artistic modernity:
critics identify the essence of painting with flatness;
sculpture, they argue, rests in peace.

§

Now to defend a bit of structure: beeline, skyline, dateline, saline—
now to torch your effluent shanty
so the small rain down can rain. I'm so Eastern that my Ph.D.
has edible tubers, my heart a hibachi oiled with rapeseed. I'm so Western that my Ph.D.

can bang and bank all ball game, bringing the crowd to its feet
and the critics to their knees. Politically speaking, I'm kind of an animal.
I feed the ducks duck meat in duck sauce when I walk to clown school in my clown shoes.
The Germans call me Ludwig, bearer of estrus, the northern kingdom's
professional apologist. The Germans call me Benji, the radical browser,
alcoholic groundskeeper of the Providence Little League. All readers of poetry

are Germans, are virgins. All readers of poetry sicken me. You, with your Soviet Ph.D.
and Afghan tiepin. You with your penis stuck in a bottle. And yes, of course, I sicken me,
with my endless and obvious examples
of the profound cultural mediocrity of the American bourgeoisie.

§

Beauty cannot account for how the sparkplug works.
But if the sparkplug doesn't work, it is more beautiful.
If I display a sparkplug, it is sculpture.
A sparkplug sculpture may be a real sparkplug,
but the sculpture refers to other sculptures, while the sparkplug refers
to an engine cylinder.
The word "sparkplug" is an altogether different matter.

Thus I return to the subject of the museum.
A woman is crying in the Surrealist wing.
Beauty cannot account for why the woman is crying.
But because the woman is crying, she is more beautiful.
Is the woman therefore a work of Surrealist sculpture?
A sculpture of a woman may be a real woman,
but the sculpture refers to other sculptures, while the woman refers

§

You say "ablution," I say "ablation."
You say "gloaming," I say "crepuscule."
You say "organ of copulation," I say "organ of excretion."
You say "forget-me-not," I say "scorpion grass."
While you were at tennis camp, I was finger-banged

by a six-fingered man. I replaced your dead goldfish
with another dead goldfish. I put your dad in a headlock
and your mom in a home. I ate your juicy motherfucking plums.

Irreconcilable differences: you disliked the Richter show.
Your gait is characterized by an exaggerated flexion of the knee.

I really don't want to do this over the phone.
But I also never want to see you again.
So I paid Ben Lerner to write you this poem
in language that was easy to understand.

§

To attend carefully to Celan in the airport terminal.
To admire the aspen in the atrium. This adjective
for that anguish. The unnatural attitudes
of the sleeping tourist. Remember

the '80s? We hit rewind
and the snow refused the ground.
We were all of us speaking German,
we were all of us wearing licensed sport apparel.

Some took your absence in stride. Some took it
lying down. Some took it with milk
and sugar. Only your wife took it like a man.

My flight originated in Denver.
My flight is now boarding. My flight is now slowly
pushing away from the gate.

§

To assimilate sculpture to sepulture, sublimity to sublation,
to ululate sub judice, to inurn in utero,
as if the absence of birds in the poem were the absence of birds in the world,
as if et cetera were an aesthetics. Ad interim,
shadows cast shadows ad infinitum. Ad absurdum,

eye-contact counts as coitus, neologism as parturition.
To squander the mind's ultimate candela on the mimetic.
To simply hurl paint at the canvas
as if it were a blackbody absorbing incident radiants,
as if in vino veritas quod erat demonstrandum nonsense as death wish,
nonsense as warm-blooded egg-laying winged and feathered vertebrate.

Now with handicap access to the principal texts,
principal texts posthumously signed.
Now with expanded signature in bilingual remission.

§

The left hand is a scandal. And my woman is left-handed.
She neglects our middle children.
She deploys her powers on behalf of other nations.
Sleep is a synagogue. And my woman sleeps
the dreamless sleep of the pornographer. Mother always said,

"Worship me, and all this will be yours." Father always said,
"Suffer common hardship and die in bed."
Yet I reside with my woman on her acre of irony.
Yet I will die on the cross and I worship my death.

The Internet is the future. And my woman rejects the Internet.
She rises up when I lie down.
She inflames divisions among the Jews.
Citation is exaltation. And my woman cites
her own unpublished dissertation.

§

I posit the notion of progress so I can experience decline.
I sport my underwear on the outside of my trousers.
My hybrid form has become a genre in its own right.
I squander my disposable income on redundant social services.
After the dissolution of feudal society, moonlight emerges

as the symbolic locus of heroic individualism.
I transform absurd contingency into historical necessity with box wine.
My facility with parataxis makes me respected, feared.
I send my professor thirty dollars' worth of fusiform compound umbels
after her only child is shot and killed. Interwar experiments with collage

reflect increasing disenchantment with the sensible world.
A wasp attacks me using her ovipositor as a sting.
I strike a teenager with a baseball bat to gain blue-collar credibility.
I feel dirty reading on the toilet.

§

I place a terminal raceme of fragrant, funnel-shaped perianths
beside the mile marker where Orlando flipped his Honda.
I fuck his girlfriend and induce epistaxis in his homeboy.

You asked me to explain the peculiar power of continental literary criticism,
to clarify what I mean by "theory" in the sentence
"To clarify what I mean by *theory* in the sentence."

The impossibility of referring to the interruption immanent in the referential chain.
Snowfall in North Topeka.
The impossibility of not referring to the immanent interruption.
Real persons, living or dead, resembled coincidentally.

Orlando imbued my body with erotic significance
by beating it with a pistol. Nothing is as metaphysical
as the claim to break from metaphysics. At a party in his honor,
we throw our hands in the air. We wave them like we just don't care.

§

Then bullets tore through the soft tissue of our episteme.
We had thought that by arranging words at random
we could avoid ideology. We were right.
Then we were terribly wrong. Such is the nature of California.

What I remember most about the Renaissance
is that everything had tits. Streetcars, sunsets,
everything. Defacing a medium
just for the F of it—
that was my idea. It was 1865;
no one was worried about positivism.

You can argue with our methods
but not with our methodology.
So a couple of janitors lost their legs.
Today, some of my best friends are janitors.

§

"Is this seat taken?" I don't understand the question.

"Was there ever any doubt?" Below the knees.

"Can you forgive me?" I hardly even know you.

"Does it have meat in it?" I'm not at liberty to say.

"Am I going to be OK?" Yes and no.

"How long was I asleep?" That remains to be seen.

"Have you met my mother?" I won't dignify that with an answer.

"Do you love me?"

"Which would you prefer?" Long ago.

"Can you hear me?" In the pejorative sense.

"How do I know it's really you?" Not exactly.

"Did you do the reading?" I do not love you.

"Swear on your life?" Swear on my life.

"Do you want me to leave?" Little by little.

§

King of Beers, King of Pop, King of Kings;
proud sponsor of rain dance and mercy killing,
Special Olympiad and circumcision;
moviegoer, meat eater, Republican: bless

my girlfriend, bless each chicken finger, the commute
to Brooklyn, watch over her hard drive and suspicious mole,
forgive her smoking, protect her from anthrax
and obesity, Scud and Rohypnol. If she is groped at a bar,
if she is cursed by a cabbie, if she loses her job,

repeal the moon, send a plague through nicotine patch
and cell phone, empty your seven bowls on the G7,
numb the penis, crash an airliner into the North Star. Destroy
with fire, short sword, and sulfur, then destroy
fire, short sword, and sulfur. Destroy me. Then destroy her.

§

In those days partial nudity was permitted
provided the breasts in question hung from indigenes.

The clouds had an ease of diction,
and Death had a way with women,
and at night our documents opened
to emit their redolent confessions.

In those days whole onions, whole peoples were immersed
in the pellucid, semisolid fat of hogs.

The children ran lines of powdered gold,
huffed glue composed of studs,
smoked burial myrrh, and then shot up
their schools.

In those days police hauled in all bugs, then birds, then stars,
and the sky fled underground.

§

Idle elevators of grain. Plenty of parking. Deciduous trees
of the genus *Ulmus,* known for their arching branches and serrate leaves
with asymmetrical bases. Gunplay in our houses of steak,
houses of pancakes. Dried valerian rhizomes. Bunk weed. Osage.

Deliberately elliptical poetic works reflect a fear of political commitment after 1968.
A fear of deliberately elliptical poetic works reflects...

Home considered as a system of substitutions: "Plenty of parking.
Deciduous elevators of the genus *Gunplay,*
known for their arching bases and serrate pancakes
with asymmetrical rhizomes." The activation of the white space of the page

reflects a fear of the industrialization of print media.
To fear the activation of the white space of the page

is to fear poetry.
Idle elliptical commitment. Deciduous repetition. Plenty of parking.

§

Blood on the time that we have on our hands.
Blood on our sheets, our sheets of music.
Blood on the canvases
of boxing rings, the canvases of Henri Matisse.

The man-child faints at the sight of blood
and so must close his eyes
as he dispatches his terrier
with a pocketknife. Tonight,

blood condensed from atmospheric vapor
falls to the earth. It bleeds three inches.
Concerts are canceled, ball games delayed.
In galoshes and slickers, the children play.

An arc of seven spectral colors appears opposite the sun
as a result of light refracted through the drops of blood.

§

The author gratefully acknowledges the object world.
Acknowledgment is gratefully made
to *Sleep: A Journal of Sleep.*
The author wishes to thank the foundation,
which poured its money into the sky.
A grant from the sky made this project impossible.

Lerner, Benjamin, 1979–1945
  The Lichtenberg figures / Benjamin Lerner.
      p. cm.
  ISBN 1-55659-211-6 (pbk. : alk. paper)
  I. Title.
  PS2343.E23432A6 1962
  911'.01–dc43   52-28544
  CIP

§

My death was first runner-up at the 1996 Kansas State Wrestling Championships (157 lbs).
My death is the author of *César Vallejo: The Complete Posthumous Poetry*.
My death was the first death in my family
to ever graduate from college.
My death graduated from the University of California, Berkeley.

Your death was the 1996 Kansas State Wrestling Champion (157 lbs).
Your death is the author of César Vallejo's *Trilce*.
Your death was the third death in your family
to deliver a commencement address
at the University of California, Berkeley.

Her death doesn't care about your death's fame or physique.
Her death is the author of *Tungsten*, César Vallejo's social-realist experiment.
Her death likes to run her hands through what's left of my death's hair.
Her death would like to start a family.

§

She left town. Rain ensued. Crows pecked out my contacts.
I tried everything: Prozac, plainsong. I won her back.
It didn't help. I shot myself. It didn't help.
A beauty incommensurate with syntax
had whupped my cracker ass.

When I was fair and young and favor graced me
my fingers were in everybody's mouth.
Ten fat fingers in ten fat mouths.
Now my fingers just point stuff out.

She shot herself. And, with a typically raucous cry,
her glossy, black body fell from the typical sky.
It fell like rain. It was rain. Fat drops of rain rained down
into my fat awaiting mouth.
It didn't help.

§

In my culture, when a woman dies, we sleep on the floor.
We sleep with her sister. We put her cats to sleep.
We tear at our hair. We tear at the hair of others.
We pass roseate urinary calculi. We dream ourselves hoarse.

In my culture, when a woman dies,
we mash the effervescent abdomens of fireflies
into mascara for the long-lashed corpse.

Virga is customary. Light opera is customary.
An exchange of fluids, of fire, is customary. It is customary to spike
the Berry Blue Kool-Aid with cyanide. Customarily,
starlings collide. And yes, of course,

after the potluck, when we've put the children to sleep,
we bathe the widower in lilac, dress him in bombazine,
and reduce him to ash.

§

The light lines up to die. The light dies down.
Out of embarrassment, the light dies out.
At 7:32 CST, the light is pronounced dead.
The light's death is pronounced

"Ayúdame."

The first female president was César Vallejo.
César Vallejo was the first African American in space.
Indicted child pornographer, César Vallejo.
Vallejo, aka Eshleman, aka Lerner.

Perdóname.

The endless miserable progression of Thursdays.
Miserable progression of glottal stops.
That "palindrome" is not a palindrome.
Endless miserable progression of decimals.

§

In the early '00s, my concern with abstraction
culminated in a series of public exhalations.
I was praised for my use of repetition. But, alas,
my work was understood.

Then the towers collapsed
and antimissile missiles tracked
the night sky with ellipses.

I decided that what we needed was a plain style,
not more condoms stuffed with chocolate frosting.
After six months in my studio, I emerged
and performed a series of public exhalations.

Only time will tell
if my work is representational.
Only time will tell if time will tell.

§

It is always already winter.
Raccoons open each other for warmth.
The poor live under the bridge outside of time.
If we can speak of the poor. If you can call that a bridge.
At a fashionable retrospective, a woman soils her prewar dress.

In order to avoid saying "I," the author eats incessantly.
The author experiences pleasure from a great distance,
like the bombing of an embassy. In the business district,
fire is exchanged. The media butcher the suspect's name.

Every weekend, the law gets laid,
while these abstractions, hung like horses,
attend their semiformals stag. The last census

counts several selves inhabiting this gaze,
mostly unemployed.

§

Forgotten in advance, these failures are technological
in the oldest sense: they allow us to see ourselves as changed
and to remain unchanged. These failures grant us

an unwelcome reprieve
and now we must celebrate wildly
until we are bereft.

As in, "Beauty rears her ugly head."
As in, "I broke her arm so I could sign the cast."

There is suffering somewhere else,
but here in Kansas our acquaintances
rape us tenderly and remain unchanged.

Will these failures grow precious through repetition
and, although we cannot hope to be forgiven,
will these failures grow precious through repetition?

§

I did it for the children. I did it for the money.
I did it for the depression of spirit and the cessation of hope.
I did it because I could, because it was there.
I'd do it again. Oops, I did it again.

What have I done? What have I done
to deserve this? What have I done with my keys,
my youth? What am I going to do
while you're at tennis camp? What are we going to do

with the body? I don't do smack. I don't do
toilets. I don't do well at school. I could do
with a bath. Unto others, I do
injurious, praiseworthy, parroted acts.

Let's just do Chinese. Just do as I say. Just do me.
That does it. Easy does it. That'll do.

§

The sky narrates snow. I narrate my name in the snow.
Snow piled in paragraphs. Darkling snow. Geno-snow
and pheno-snow. I staple snow to the ground.

In medieval angelology, there are nine orders of snow.
A vindication of snow in the form of snow.
A jealous snow. An omni-snow. Snow immolation.

Do you remember that winter it snowed?
There were bodies everywhere. Obese, carrot-nosed.
A snow of translucent hexagonal signifiers. Meta-snow.

Sand replaced with snow. Snowpaper. A window of snow
opened onto the snow. Snow replaced with sand.
A sandman. Obese, carrot-nosed. Tiny swastikas

of snow. Vallejo's unpublished snow.
Real snow on the stage. Fake blood on the snow.

ABOUT THE AUTHOR

Ben Lerner is originally from Topeka, Kansas. He holds degrees in political theory and creative writing from Brown University, and his poems have appeared in a variety of literary magazines, including *The Paris Review*, *Ploughshares*, and *The Threepenny Review*. He co-edits *No: a journal of the arts*, and was awarded a 2003–2004 Fulbright Scholarship to Spain.

Copper Canyon Press wishes to acknowledge the support of Lannan Foundation in funding the publication and distribution of exceptional literary works.

LANNAN LITERARY SELECTIONS 2004

Marvin Bell, *Rampant*
Cyrus Cassells, *More Than Peace and Cypresses*
Ben Lerner, *The Lichtenberg Figures*
Joseph Stroud, *Country of Light*
Eleanor Rand Wilner, *The Girl with Bees in Her Hair*

LANNAN LITERARY SELECTIONS 2000–2003

John Balaban, *Spring Essence: The Poetry of Hồ Xuân Hương,*

Hayden Carruth, *Doctor Jazz*

Norman Dubie, *The Mercy Seat: Collected & New Poems, 1967–2001*

Sascha Feinstein, *Misterioso*

James Galvin, *X: Poems*

Jim Harrison, *The Shape of the Journey: New and Collected Poems*

Maxine Kumin, *Always Beginning: Essays on a Life in Poetry*

Antonio Machado, *Border of a Dream: Selected Poems,* translated by Willis Barnstone

W.S. Merwin, *The First Four Books of Poems*

Cesare Pavese, *Disaffections: Complete Poems 1930–1950,* translated by Geoffrey Brock

Antonio Porchia, *Voices,* translated by W.S. Merwin

Kenneth Rexroth, *The Complete Poems of Kenneth Rexroth,* edited by Sam Hamill and Bradford Morrow

Alberto Ríos, *The Smallest Muscle in the Human Body*

Theodore Roethke, *On Poetry & Craft*

Ann Stanford, *Holding Our Own: The Selected Poems of Ann Stanford,* edited by Maxine Scates and David Trinidad

Ruth Stone, *In the Next Galaxy*

Rabindranath Tagore, *The Lover of God,* translated by Tony K. Stewart and Chase Twichell

Reversible Monuments: Contemporary Mexican Poetry, edited by Mónica de la Torre and Michael Wiegers

César Vallejo, *The Black Heralds,* translated by Rebecca Seiferle

C.D. Wright, *Steal Away: Selected and New Poems*

For more on the Lannan Literary Selections,
visit: www.coppercanyonpress.org

The Chinese character for poetry is made up of two parts: "word" and "temple." It also serves as pressmark for Copper Canyon Press.

Founded in 1972, Copper Canyon Press remains dedicated to publishing poetry exclusively, from Nobel laureates to new and emerging authors. The Press thrives with the generous patronage of readers, writers, booksellers, librarians, teachers, students, and funders—everyone who shares the conviction that poetry invigorates the language and sharpens our appreciation of the world.

Major funding has been provided by:
The Allen Foundation for The Arts
Lannan Foundation
National Endowment for the Arts
The Starbucks Foundation
Washington State Arts Commission

For information and catalogs:
COPPER CANYON PRESS
Post Office Box 271
Port Townsend, Washington 98368
360/385-4925
www.coppercanyonpress.org

Printed in the USA
CPSIA information can be obtained
at www.ICGtesting.com
JSHW050822010923
47221JS00001B/1